Leaving My Homeland

A Refugee's Journey from Iraq

Ellen Rodger

CRABTREE Publishing Company
www.crabtreebooks.com

Crabtree Publishing Company
www.crabtreebooks.com

Author: Ellen Rodger

Editorial director: Kathy Middleton

Editors: Sarah Eason, Kelly Spence, and Janine Deschenes

Design: Jessica Moon

Cover design: Jessica Moon

Photo research: Rachel Blount

Proofreader: Wendy Scavuzzo

Production coordinator and prepress technician: Ken Wright

Print coordinator: Margaret Amy Salter

Consultants: Hawa Sabriye and HaEun Kim,
Centre for Refugee Studies, York University

Publisher's Note: The story presented in this book
is a fictional account based on extensive research
of real-life accounts by refugees with the aim to reflect the
true experience of refugee children and their families.

Written and produced for Crabtree Publishing Company
by Calcium Creative

Photo Credits:
t=Top, bl=Bottom Left, br=Bottom Right

Shutterstock: Artskvortsova: p. 14bl; Andrey Bayda: p. 22–23;
Brothers Good: p. 6br; Orhan Cam: p. 14br; Cloud Mine
Amsterdam: p. 24–25b; Fotokon: p. 19; Eng. Bilal Izaddin:
pp. 4c, 6bl; Anjo Kan: p. 21; A katz:
p. 27; Aman Ahmed Khan: p. 8; Thomas Koch: p. 7t; Ivan
Kotliar: p. 21b; Lawkeeper: p. 25b; Macrovector: pp. 3, 4t, 5b,
16t, 17t, 22t, 25br; Svetlana Maslova: p. 16b; Mclek:
p. 22–23b; MSSA: pp. 13t, 15t, 29tl; Northfoto: pp. 10t, 10b;
Angela Ostafichuk: p. 24–25t; Owen_Holdaway: pp. 12, 13;
Angela N Perryman: p. 14c; Andrew Rybalko: p. 10b; Seita:
p. 12–13b; Stoker-13: p. 18l; Suronin: pp. 18, 20c; Melih Cevdet
Teksen: p. 16c; Globe Turner: p. 5tr; Txking: p. 29tr; Jim Vallee:
pp. 5t, 9t, 15; What's My Name: p. 20t; Wikimedia Commons:
Dane Hillard: p. 26; U.S. Marine Corps: p. 11t; Rachel Unkovic/
International Rescue Committee: pp. 11b, 17b.

Cover: Shutterstock: Svetlana Maslova (right), Prazis (bottom).

Library and Archives Canada Cataloguing in Publication

Rodger, Ellen, author
    A refugee's journey from Iraq / Ellen Rodger.

(Leaving my homeland)
Includes index.
Issued in print and electronic formats.
ISBN 978-0-7787-3127-6 (hardcover).--ISBN 978-0-7787-3157-3 (softcover).--
ISBN 978-1-4271-1880-6 (HTML)

    1. Refugees--Iraq--Juvenile literature. 2. Refugees--United States--
Juvenile literature. 3. Refugee children--Iraq--Juvenile literature.
4. Refugee children--United States--Juvenile literature. 5. Refugees--Social
conditions--Juvenile literature. 6. Iraq--Social conditions--Juvenile
literature. I. Title.

HV640.5.I76R63 2017   j305.9'06914095670973   C2016-907091-3
                                                       C2016-907092-1

Library of Congress Cataloging-in-Publication Data

Names: Rodger, Ellen, author.
Title: A refugee's journey from Iraq / written by Ellen Rodger.
Description: New York, N.Y. : Crabtree Publishing Company, 2017. |
    Series: Leaving my homeland | Includes index.
Identifiers: LCCN 2016054843 (print) | LCCN 2016059637 (ebook) |
    ISBN 9780778731276 (reinforced library binding : alk. paper) |
    ISBN 9780778731573 (pbk : alk. paper) |
    ISBN 9781427118806 (Electronic HTML)
Subjects: LCSH: Refugees--Iraq--Juvenile literature. | Refugees--Michigan--
    Juvenile literature. | Refugee children--Iraq--Juvenile literature. | Refugee
    children--Michigan--Juvenile literature. | Refugees--Social conditions--Juvenile
    literature. | Iraq--Social conditions--21st century--Juvenile literature.
Classification: LCC HV640.5.I76 R63 2017 (print) | LCC HV640.5.I76 (ebook) |
    DDC 362.7/791409567--dc23
LC record available at https://lccn.loc.gov/2016054843

Crabtree Publishing Company
www.crabtreebooks.com   1-800-387-7650

Printed in Canada/022017/CH20161214

Published in Canada
Crabtree Publishing
616 Welland Ave.
St. Catharines, ON
L2M 5V6

Published in the United States
Crabtree Publishing
PMB 59051
350 Fifth Avenue, 59th Floor
New York, New York 10118

Published in the United Kingdom
Crabtree Publishing
Maritime House
Basin Road North, Hove
BN41 1WR

Published in Australia
Crabtree Publishing
3 Charles Street
Coburg North
VIC, 3058

What Is in This Book?

Leaving Iraq

There has been war and conflict in Iraq for a very long time. Many Iraqi children do not know of a time when there was peace. They were born during conflict. For some, their parents were also born during war.

Many Iraqi children, such as this boy in Kirkuk, become orphans when their families are killed in areas of conflict.

UN Rights of the Child

Every child has **rights**. Rights are privileges and freedoms that are protected by law. **Refugees** have the right to special protection and help. The United Nations (UN) Convention on the Rights of the Child is a document that lists the rights of children all over the world. Think about these rights as you read this book.

Iraq has experienced almost 60 years of unstable governments, conflicts, wars, and **terrorism**. There have been times of peace, too. Even after the most recent war ended in 2011, fighting has continued between the Iraqi army, **militias**, and **insurgent groups**. Many cities and villages have become battlegrounds.

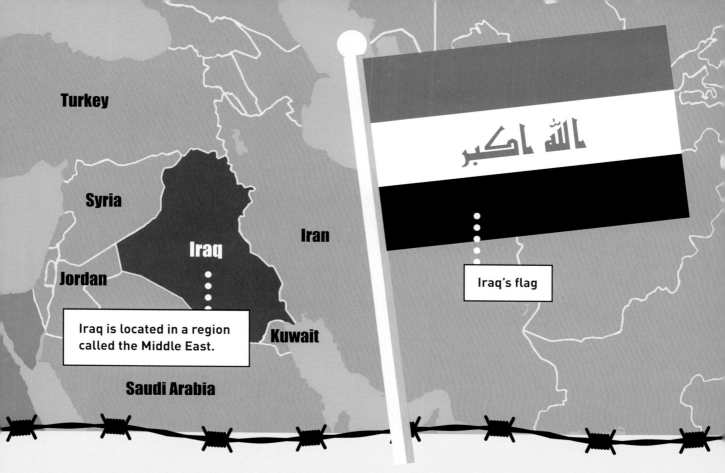

Turkey

Syria

Jordan

Iraq

الله اكبر

Iraq is located in a region called the Middle East.

Iran

Kuwait

Saudi Arabia

Iraq's flag

Some people remain in Iraq but are forced from their homes. They are **internally displaced persons (IDPs)**. Refugees are people who flee their **homeland** to find safety in another country, often because of conflict. Other people move to new countries to look for better opportunities for themselves and their children. These people are **immigrants**.

People have been leaving Iraq for many years. While there are a number of camps for displaced persons in the country, many Iraqis have settled in nearby countries as **temporary** residents. Some hope to return to their homeland when it is safe.

My Homeland, Iraq

Thousands of years ago, Iraq was home to some of the earliest human settlements. They developed along the banks of the Tigris River and Euphrates River. These two rivers wind through Iraq from north to south.

The first writing system, called cuneiform (kyoo-NEE-uh-fawrm), developed in Iraq in 400 B.C.E. Medicine, astronomy, math, and written laws were also developed there. Objects from that time can still be found in Iraq. Sadly, many have been stolen or destroyed during the recent wars and conflicts.

Baghdad is the capital of Iraq.

● Baghdad

Tigris

Euphrates

The Tigris is the second-longest river in Iraq, after the Euphrates.

People from many different religions and cultures call Iraq home. Most Iraqis are **Muslim**. Muslims follow the Islamic faith and the teachings of the prophet Muhammad. Iraq also has ethnic groups who speak their own languages and follow their own traditions.

Most Iraqi people are Arabs. Kurds live mostly in the northern region of Kurdistan. Arabic and Kurdish are the official languages of Iraq. Many other languages are spoken there, too.

A mosque is a Muslim house of worship. The two tall towers on this mosque in Karbala are called minarets (min-uh-RETS).

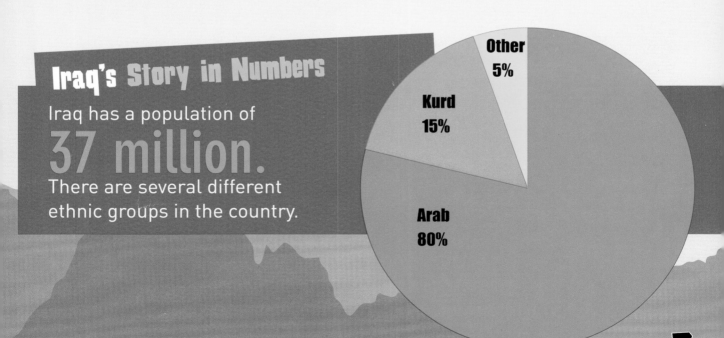

Iraq's Story in Numbers

Iraq has a population of

37 million.

There are several different ethnic groups in the country.

Other 5%

Kurd 15%

Arab 80%

Zainab's Story: My Life Before the War

Before the war, my family lived in a nice house in Baghdad. My mother worked for a doctor and my father was a **translator**. He speaks and writes very good English. My sisters, Aisha and Mariam, went to a good school.

I was born in 2003, the year the war started. During the war, my father worked as an English translator for an American company. After a bomb exploded near our house, my father sent my mother, my sisters, and me to Ramadi to live with my grandparents. He thought we would be safer there.

Like many Iraqi women, this girl wears a head scarf called a hijab when in public.

UN Rights of the Child

You have the right to protection and freedom from war.

My father continued to work in Baghdad. Soon there was fighting and bombing in Ramadi, too. One day, the soldiers arrested my grandfather. But they let him go. They would come into the house and yell and look for things, mostly at night. We slept with our clothes on so that if the soldiers came to take us, we would be dressed.

My grandfather was sick during the war. My mother and grandmother looked after him, but there was not much medicine. When he passed away, my uncles buried him. My uncle Qusay lived with us. He helped take care of me and my sisters. When my father came to Ramadi after the war, he was scared. A militia had left a note on our apartment door. The note called him a **traitor** for working with the Americans. It said he would be killed for helping the enemy.

During the Iraq War, food and other goods became very expensive in Iraq.

The Iraqi Conflict

Saddam Hussein remained in power for more than 20 years. He is shown praying in this mural in Baghdad.

For many years, Iraq was ruled by the **Ottoman Empire**. After the Ottomans lost power, Britain took control of the country. Iraq gained **independence** in 1932. By 1979, a man named Saddam Hussein controlled the country.

Hussein was a **dictator**. His rule lasted until 2003. He was both loved and hated by the Iraqi people. Iraq has lots of oil, which is very valuable. Hussein used the wealth from the oil to build and modernize the country. Under his rule, Iraq experienced many years of conflict.

Iraq's Story in Numbers

Iraq is one of the most oil-rich countries in the world. In 2014, the country produced more than

3 million

barrels of oil per day.

In 1980, Hussein invaded Iran, starting an eight-year war. Ten years later, his forces entered Kuwait to take the country's oil. This started the first Gulf War (1990–1991) between Iraq and the United States. In 2003, the United States demanded that Hussein leave Iraq. When he refused, the United States and other countries invaded Iraq. Hussein was captured and put on trial for crimes against the Iraqi people. He was **executed** in 2006.

During the Iraq War, American troops occupied Baghdad. Saddam Hussein fled and the Americans helped train a new Iraqi army.

The Iraq War created chaos. There was fighting between cultural and religious groups, and the new American-trained Iraqi army. **Civil war** broke out. An **extremist** group called the **Islamic State in Iraq and the Levant (ISIL)** began taking over cities and villages. ISIL wants to rule Iraq. They control a large part of the country, as well as parts of Syria to the west. ISIL fights with the Iraqi army and local militias. Foreign countries are also fighting ISIL. Many refugees fleeing the violence now live in camps. Others are trapped in parts of Iraq under ISIL control.

The Yazidi are a Kurdish ethnic group from northern Iraq. Many Yazidi families have fled from their homes in areas under ISIL control.

Fleeing to Safety

When cities are bombed, Iraqis try to stay safe in their homes. They collect food, clean water, and fuel. They use these supplies to survive when it is too dangerous to leave their homes.

Millions of people in Iraq are internally displaced. They have fled their homes because of the fighting. Many walk for several hours to safety. Some live with family in other parts of the country. Others stay in camps set up by aid organizations such as the United Nations (UN). The UN is made up of many countries. It works to solve problems and helps people in need.

In September 2015, the Rwanga camp in northern Iraq housed more than 15,000 IDPs.

Iraq's Story in Numbers

In 2016, more than **268,000** people fled their homes in ISIL-controlled areas of Iraq. **One third** of Iraq's population is in need of aid.

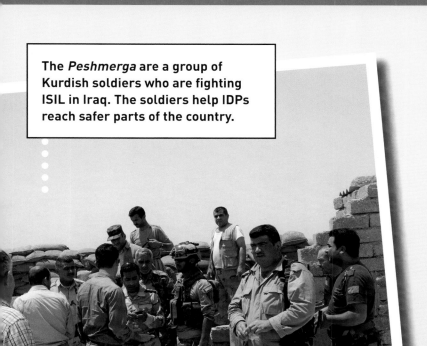

The *Peshmerga* are a group of Kurdish soldiers who are fighting ISIL in Iraq. The soldiers help IDPs reach safer parts of the country.

ISIL controls areas in the northern and western parts of Iraq, near Syria. People who live in these areas flee at night to avoid ISIL soldiers. In 2014, ISIL took over Mosul, the second-largest city in Iraq. Many camps were built for people fleeing the city. Thousands more were trapped in Mosul. They were caught in the middle of the fighting between ISIL and the Iraqi army.

Zainab's Story: Leaving Ramadi

It was not safe to go back to Baghdad. There was no water or electricity at our house. Most of our neighbors were gone. Many buildings were destroyed. My father was on a list of people the militia wanted to kill. My father and mother are brave and strong. They made a plan for us to escape.

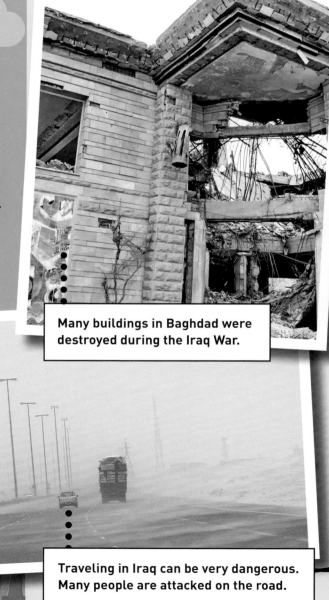

Many buildings in Baghdad were destroyed during the Iraq War.

Traveling in Iraq can be very dangerous. Many people are attacked on the road.

We wanted to bring my grandmother, but she did not want to leave. Qusay and my other relatives lived nearby. They would look after each other. Before we left, we prayed and had a family meal. I played with my cousins. My father told me to be brave.

We drove to Jordan. My father had our passports and papers ready. The border guards let us into the country as visitors. I think I was too young to be scared. But my mother and sisters were scared. They knew how dangerous it would be if we were turned away.

We arrived in Amman, the capital of Jordan. There, we **registered** with the United Nations High Commissioner for Refugees (UNHCR). It is the branch of the UN that helps refugees. They gave us **asylum**-seeker cards to show that we were refugees who left Iraq because our lives were in danger. This allowed us to stay, but not forever.

UN Rights of the Child

Children have the right to food, clothing, and a safe place to live.

Where Do People Go?

IDPs in Iraq and refugees in camps in other countries live very difficult lives. Camps are often crowded. Many are in the desert. It is very hot in the summer and very cold in the winter. There is little food, water, and medicine. In the winter, warm clothing and heaters are needed.

It is a challenge to provide food, water, and shelter for all of the people who need help.

Iraqis line up to receive food and water in camps. Each person is given a specific amount of food, called a ration.

In 2016, more than

3.3 million

Iraqis were internally displaced.

It costs a lot of money to provide for refugees. There is often not enough supplies for everyone. In some camps, rations are cut back so that everyone has something to eat. Aid organizations require more donations to meet the demands of the Iraqi crisis.

Many fellow Iraqis also help people who are fleeing. Bahari Taza is a small village in northern Iraq. More than 600 families have fled to a camp in the village set up by Adnan Mohammed Ali, a community leader. Local families volunteer to cook and deliver food. They also give money to buy supplies for people living in the camp.

When people arrive in camps, they register. This helps aid organizations know how much food and other resources are needed.

Zainab's Story: Safe in Amman

Amman is a big, modern city. There are millions of people and many shopping malls. We lived in a small apartment. It was not very nice. I slept on the floor with my sisters. Some days, we did not eat because we had no money to buy food.

About 90 percent of Iraqi refugees in Jordan settle in Amman and the surrounding area.

As refugees, my parents were not allowed to work in Jordan. My father sold everything he could to have enough money for us. We also borrowed money from family. My father sometimes worked **illegally**, building apartment buildings.

At first we could not go to school. We had arrived in the middle of the year. When we were able to go to school, I was happy. Aisha did not go to school often. She stayed home to look after our mother and the apartment.

All children are allowed to go to school in Jordan, no matter where they are from.

One day, we met with people from the UNHCR office in Amman. We were told that we could apply for asylum in the United States because my father had worked for an American company during the war.

We met with people from the American government. We were asked lots of questions. My parents had to fill out many forms. It was frightening, but exciting, too. If we could go to the United States, we would be safe. I used to dream about America. What would it be like there?

It was a happy day when we were accepted as refugees in America. Our family would have a fresh start. But even after we heard the good news, it was more than a year before we left Jordan.

Life on the Move

Many Iraqis who flee become **urban** refugees in neighboring countries. This means they live in cities and villages instead of refugee camps. Urban refugees must pay for housing, food, medicine, and schooling. Not all can afford it. Some receive help from aid organizations. Aid organizations give money, or supply food and clothing.

Iraqi refugees are not always welcomed in other Arabic countries. They are blamed for high costs of housing and food. People are afraid the refugees will take jobs. But this is not true. Most refugees cannot legally work. Food is hard to find and people may not eat every day. If refugees work illegally, they risk being sent back to Iraq.

Some refugees receive coupons from aid organizations that can be exchanged for food at local markets.

UN Rights of the Child

You have the right to help from the government if you are poor or in need.

Iraqi refugees who reach Europe land on the rocky shores of Greece. There, they live in refugee camps before journeying farther into Europe.

Many Iraqi refugees live in neighboring countries for years. Others travel on to try to reach Europe. They make the dangerous journey across the Mediterranean Sea in small boats. Those who make it hope to receive asylum in Europe, North America, Australia, and other countries. Organizations such as the UN help people apply for refugee **resettlement** programs. Not many are accepted.

Zainab's Story: Jordan to Michigan

We waited for many years. Eventually we were told we could go to the United States. My father taught us to speak English. Aisha found it hard. Mariam and I studied for many hours each day. I wanted to know everything.

We were very happy to leave Jordan. We could have a fresh start in the United States, and we would finally be safe. We were sad because we might not see our family in Iraq ever again. I would never again play with my cousins. I would never again eat klicha (date cookies) at my grandmother's house.

United States

Jordan

UN Rights of the Child

You have the right to find out things and share what you think with others, by talking, drawing, writing, or in any other way, unless it harms or offends other people.

Many refugees start their new lives in large cities. These places often have Arabic communities, and offer more opportunities for refugees to find work and housing.

We flew in an airplane to our new home in Michigan. It was very exciting. But I could tell my parents were nervous. We knew only one person in Michigan. He is my father's cousin. I like the name Michigan. Mariam said it sounds like freedom.

Our plane landed in Detroit. It is a big city on a river. It is bigger than Ramadi, but different from Amman. There are many roads and cars here. We arrived in the fall. The trees were so colorful. In Iraq, there is desert. Here it is wet. It rains a lot. In the winter, it snows sometimes.

Challenges Refugees Face

Refugees arriving in a new country often feel like outsiders. This may affect how they act. In their home country, the government, police, or army might be **corrupt**. It can be difficult for them to fully trust people. It may reassure them to be around people from their own country and culture. But refugees also like to learn about their new home and its way of life.

It is hard to prepare for living in a new country. Refugees may not speak the same language as everyone else. Some refugee children may not have been in school for years. Children and their parents may suffer from having experienced conflict.

Many refugees from Iraq form tightly knit communities in the countries where they settle.

In many countries, people hold peaceful protests to encourage their governments to help refugees.

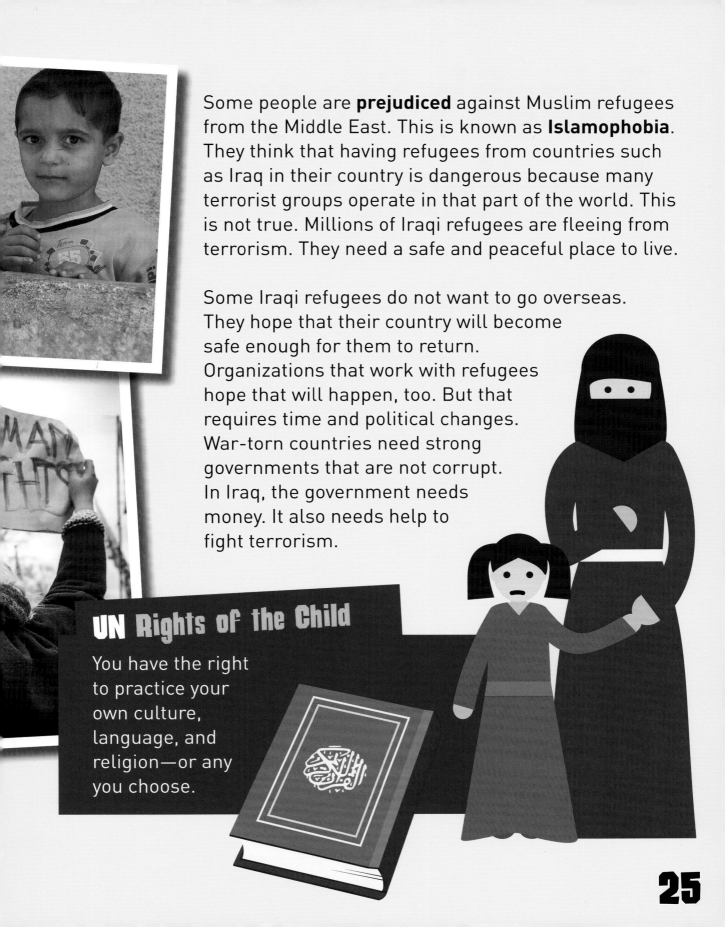

Some people are **prejudiced** against Muslim refugees from the Middle East. This is known as **Islamophobia**. They think that having refugees from countries such as Iraq in their country is dangerous because many terrorist groups operate in that part of the world. This is not true. Millions of Iraqi refugees are fleeing from terrorism. They need a safe and peaceful place to live.

Some Iraqi refugees do not want to go overseas. They hope that their country will become safe enough for them to return. Organizations that work with refugees hope that will happen, too. But that requires time and political changes. War-torn countries need strong governments that are not corrupt. In Iraq, the government needs money. It also needs help to fight terrorism.

UN Rights of the Child

You have the right to practice your own culture, language, and religion—or any you choose.

Zainab's Story: My New Home in America

I am so happy in our new home in Dearborn, Michigan. I go to school and I am learning many new things. My teacher says my English is good. That is because my father takes me to the library every week. I can borrow books for free! At school, I have friends from many places. My friend Monique asked me to come to her birthday party!

Dearborn, Michigan, has a large Arabic community. The largest mosque in North America is located in Dearborn.

Mariam also goes to school with me. But Aisha only studies at night. She says school is hard here. My parents tell her she must spend more time studying because she has missed so much school.

My father works at a store. He takes classes at night to get American qualifications. Then he can work as a translator again.

There are other Iraqis here, too. There are also many people who come from other Arab countries. My mother is still sad, but she has met many other Arabs. She talks on the phone to our family back home. Ramadi was taken over by ISIL. Months later, the government army drove ISIL out. I am glad to be safe in Dearborn. My homeland is still a very dangerous place.

Iraq's Story in Numbers

Since 2006, more than

125,000

Iraqi refugees have settled in the United States. Between 2009 and 2014, almost

20,000

Iraqi refugees arrived in Canada.

There are many organizations, such as the Arab American Association of New York, that invite people from all backgrounds to learn about Arabic culture and holidays such as Eid.

You Can Help!

There are many things you can do to help refugees from places such as Iraq. Learning about another culture and putting yourself in a newcomer's position is a good place to start.

☑ Be a friend to a refugee or newcomer. Learn about their culture. Help them learn about yours.

☑ Ask your teacher if your class or school can hold an immigrant and refugee day. Celebrate World Refugee Day on June 20.

☑ Plan a fundraising event, such as a bake sale or a car wash. Ask a parent, guardian, or teacher to help. Donate the money you raise to a charity that helps Iraqi refugees and IDPs.

☑ Words have power. Write letters to local officials asking them to support giving aid to people affected by the fighting in Iraq. Speak up if you hear someone say something prejudiced about refugees.

☑ In your own life, learn to solve problems by cooperating with others and treating everyone with respect.

Iraq's Story in Numbers

More than

4.7 million

children in Iraq are affected by the ongoing conflict and are in need of aid.

HUMANITARIAN
AID

In Boise, Idaho, people gather to welcome refugees to their community.

Discussion Prompts

1. Explain the difference between a refugee and an immigrant. Give an example of how and why each come to a new country.
2. As a class, brainstorm ways you can help a refugee adjust to living in your community.

Glossary

asylum Protection or shelter from danger

civil war A war between groups of people in the same country

corrupt Dishonest; usually for personal gain

dictator A ruler who has absolute power over a country

executed Put to death

extremist Having a strong belief in something; often political

homeland The country where someone was born or grew up

illegally Against the law

immigrants People who leave one country to live in another

independence Freedom from outside control

insurgent groups Groups that try to overthrow a government, usually through violence

internally displaced persons (IDPs) People who are forced from their homes during a conflict but who remain in their country

Islamic State in Iraq and the Levant Also called ISIL; a group of extremist Muslims who believe that people who do not share their beliefs are enemies

Islamophobia A fear or dislike of Muslims

militias Military groups that are not part of a country's army

Muslim A follower of Islam

Ottoman Empire A former Turkish empire that ended in 1922

prejudiced Having an unfair dislike of someone

refugees People who flee to another country due to unsafe conditions

registered Was added to an official list

resettlement Moving people from one place to another to live

rights Privileges and freedoms protected by law

temporary Lasting a short time

terrorism The use of violence to force people to accept a point of view

traitor A person who betrays something or someone

translator A person who changes written or spoken words from one language to another

urban Relating to a city or town

Learning More

Books

Dunn, Joeming W. *Fallujah*. ABDO Publishing, 2016.

Owings, Lisa. *Exploring Iraq*. Bellwether Media, 2011.

Pipe, Jim. *Hoping for Peace in Iraq*. Gareth Stevens, 2013.

Winter, Jeanette. *The Librarian of Basra: A True Story from Iraq*. HMH Books for Young Readers, 2004.

Websites

kids.nationalgeographic.com/explore/countries/iraq/#iraq-children.jpg
Visit this site for a good overview on the history and geography of Iraq.

www.playagainstallodds.ca
Play Against All Odds, an interactive game provided by the UNHCR, takes a player through the experience of a refugee.

www.unicef.ca/sites/default/files/legacy/imce_uploads/images/advocacy/co/crc_poster_en.pdf
Explore the United Nations Convention on the Rights of the Child.

www.unicef.org/infobycountry/iraq_92964.html
Iraqi children offer insight into their experiences as refugees.

Index

About the Author

Ellen Rodger is a descendant of refugees who fled persecution and famine. She has written and edited many books for children and adults on subjects as varied as potatoes, how government works, social justice, war, soccer, and lice and fleas.